MYSTERIES
OF
METEORS, ASTEROIDS AND COMETS

by Ellen Labrecque

Raintree is an imprint of Capstone Global Library Limited, a company incorporated in England and Wales having its registered office at 264 Banbury Road, Oxford, OX2 7DY – Registered company number: 6695582

www.raintree.co.uk
myorders@raintree.co.uk

Edited by Hank Musolf
Designed by Sara Radka
Original illustrations © Capstone Global Library Limited 2021
Picture research by Jo Miller
Production by Laura Manthe
Originated by Capstone Global Library Ltd
Printed and bound in India

978 1 3982 0471 3 (hardback)
978 1 3982 0470 6 (paperback)

British Library Cataloguing in Publication Data
A full catalogue record for this book is available from the British Library.

Acknowledgements
We would like to thank the following for permission to reproduce photographs: Alamy Stock Photo: NG Images, 28; AP Images: P Video, 15; Dreamstime: Bazuzzza, 17; iStock: Marharyta Marko, 5, serpeblu, 4; NASA: ESA/ATG medialab, 13, ESA/Giotto Project, 23, ESA/STScI, 25, JPL-Caltech, 9, 27, JPL-Caltech/Teledyne, 11, JPL-Caltech/UCAL/MPS/DLR/IDA, 12, NASA Goddard, 29; Newscom: Danita Delimont Photography/David Wall, 22; Pixabay: Hans, 8; Shutterstock: abriendomundo, 19, Aygun Ali, background, Dotted Yeti, 16, faboi, 18, Johan Swanepoel, 6, solarseven, 21, Song_about_summer, 14

Every effort has been made to contact copyright holders of material reproduced in this book. Any omissions will be rectified in subsequent printings if notice is given to the publisher.

CONTENTS

Words in **bold** are in the glossary.

CHAPTER 1

SMASHING INTO EARTH

Imagine Earth 66 million years ago. The sun is shining. Dinosaurs are stomping around. An **asteroid** is hurtling towards the planet. It is the size of a mountain. It is travelling at 64,370 kilometres (40,000 miles) per hour! The asteroid looks like a giant fireball as it gets closer. It burns much hotter than the Sun. It explodes on impact. The crash is felt all over the world. The impact sends a blanket of dust into the air. The sky turns black. Soon dinosaurs are wiped out forever.

Scientists believe dinosaurs were wiped out by an asteroid.

An asteroid flies towards a planet.

Scientists believe dinosaurs died out after a large asteroid hit Earth. Today, outer space is filled with asteroids like that one. Could a rock like this hit Earth again? It could, but don't worry. The chances of a large asteroid hitting Earth are very small. People watch space objects every day to help keep us safe.

Outer space is filled with asteroids and other objects. They include small rocks called **meteoroids** and objects made of rock, ice and dust called **comets**. We know a lot about these objects, but scientists are still learning about them. They are solving mysteries about them as they learn.

MYSTERY FACT

The asteroid that scientists believe wiped out the dinosaurs was more than 9.7 km (6 miles) wide.

Rocks of different sizes fly throughout space.

Outer space is filled with flying rocks. Most **astronomers** think the **Big Bang** is the way the universe began. About 13.7 billion years ago, all the **matter** and **energy** in outer space was crammed in a small, hot place. The pressure was so intense that it finally burst. It exploded in every direction. This led to the planets, moons and stars forming. Scientists think it is also the reason we have so many rocks in space.

MYSTERY FACT

Our universe continues to expand today. When the universe grows, galaxies spread further apart. Scientists are still trying to work out how fast the universe expands.

CHAPTER 2

DEFENDING PLANET EARTH

Astronomers study space rocks. The space rocks tell the story of our universe. The ones closest to Earth are called near-Earth objects (NEOs). Over 19,000 NEOs have been discovered. More than 30 new ones are found every week. Astronomers keep track of them. Most of them are at least 48 million km (30 million miles) away, but some are closer.

Potentially hazardous objects (PHOs) are as close as 7.5 million km (4.7 million miles) away. Astronomers keep an especially close eye on PHOs.

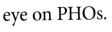

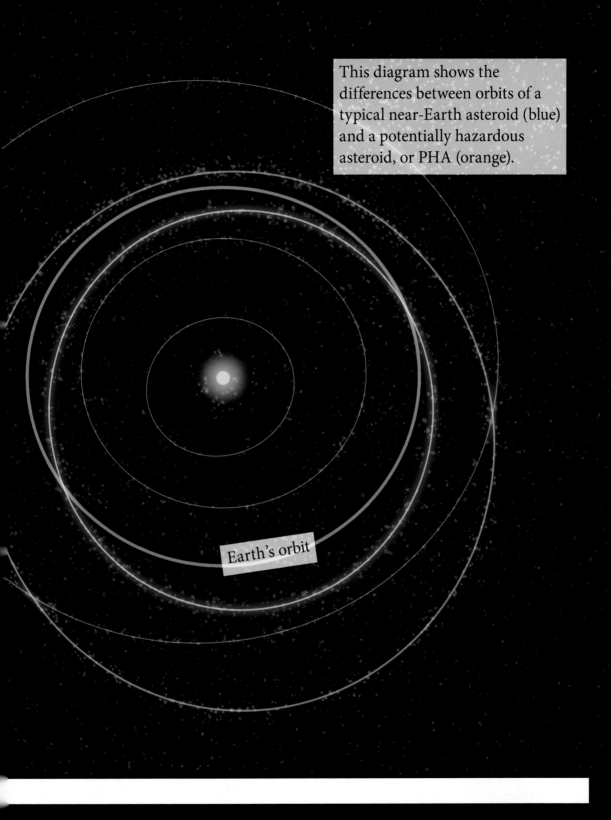

This diagram shows the differences between orbits of a typical near-Earth asteroid (blue) and a potentially hazardous asteroid, or PHA (orange).

Earth's orbit

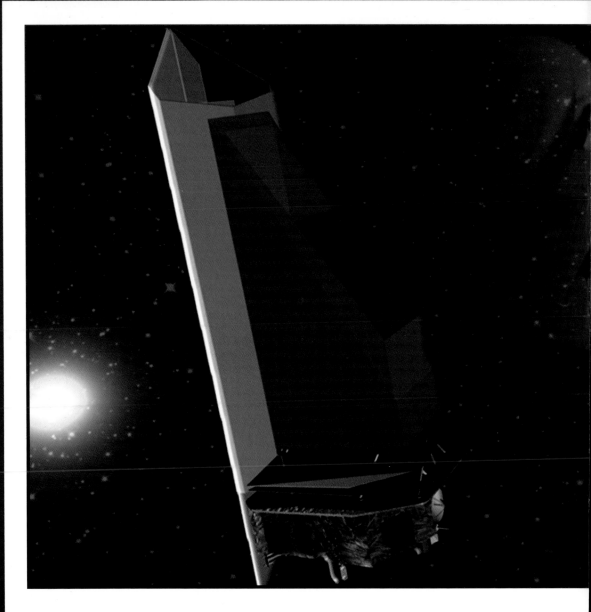

The Planetary Defense Coordination Office is one group working to keep us safe. Group members track space objects that are flying close to Earth. They are building a new asteroid-hunting **telescope** called the NEOCam. It will be ready in 2024.

The NEOCam sensor (right) is the foundation for the proposed Near Earth Object Camera, or NEOCam (left).

Asteroids give off heat against the backdrop of cold space. This telescope will be able to pick up that heat. The more we know about asteroids, the better prepared we can be.

CHAPTER 3

ASTEROIDS

Asteroids are called small planets. Like our planets, they orbit the Sun. Most asteroids can be found in the **asteroid belt**. The asteroid belt is a place between the planets Mars and Jupiter. More than 2 million asteroids are found there. The brightest asteroid in the sky is called Vesta. The biggest asteroid ever found is called Ceres. It is more than 900 km (590 miles) wide!

Vesta

Dwarf planet Ceres is located in the main asteroid belt between the orbits of Mars and Jupiter.

Asteroids crash into Earth every day. Together, the space rocks that fall daily weigh close to 91,000 kilograms (200,000 pounds). These rocks aren't the big sort that could really hurt us. Earth is surrounded by thin layers of gases. This is called the **atmosphere**. Our atmosphere serves as a shield. It breaks up asteroids into pieces. They usually reach Earth in the form of dust and small rocks.

Earth seen from space at night

Throughout Earth's long history, gigantic rocks have hit us. We have the **craters** to prove it. The biggest crater on Earth is called Vredefort Crater. It is in South Africa. It is 305 km (190 miles) wide. An asteroid created this crater 2 billion years ago. It was at least 9.6 km (6 miles) wide.

AN UNEXPECTED ASTEROID

In 2013, astronomers were caught off guard. A giant asteroid entered Earth's atmosphere above Chelyabinsk, Russia. The asteroid was 17 metres (55 feet) wide and weighed more than 11 million kg (26 million pounds). Astronomers didn't see it coming. The asteroid was bright and flying close to the Sun. Luckily, it exploded before it hit the ground. The air blast still caused damage to more than 7,000 buildings. Thankfully, nobody died.

CHAPTER 4

METEOROIDS, METEORS AND METEORITES

Asteroids and meteoroids are made of the same type of rock and metals. They are both found outside our atmosphere. A meteoroid is a much smaller asteroid. It can be as small as a pebble. Often a meteoroid is just a piece of asteroid. Two asteroids might have crashed into each other, causing pieces to break off.

asteroid

meteoroid

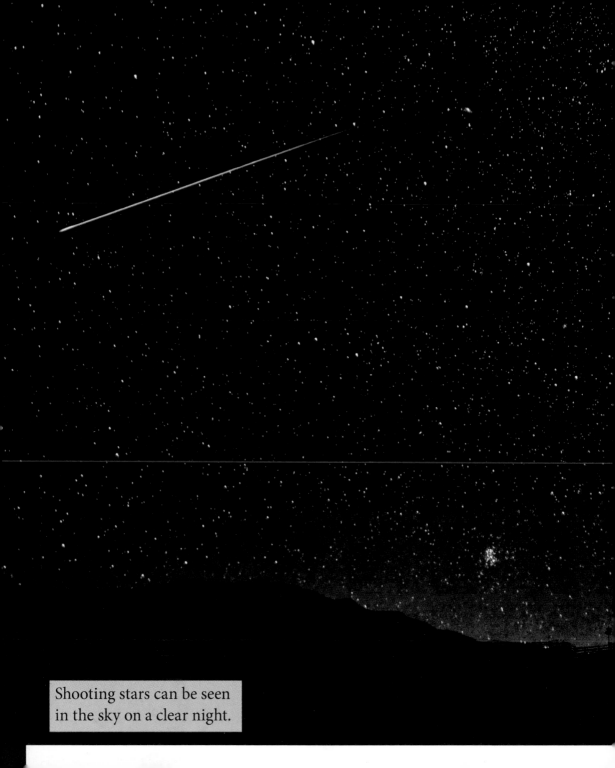

Shooting stars can be seen in the sky on a clear night.

When a meteoroid enters our atmosphere, it becomes known as a **meteor**, or a shooting star. This happens when our atmosphere can't deflect the meteoroid. Instead, it causes the meteoroid to slow down suddenly. It usually burns up before it hits the surface. This burning causes a bright streak across a dark sky. Sometimes the meteor doesn't burn up. It actually lands on Earth. What remains is called a **meteorite**. Most of the time the meteorites are so small that we don't even notice them.

meteorite

CHAPTER 5

COMETS

Comets are another type of space object. Comets form far away from the Sun. They are made up of ice, dust and rock. Comets are nicknamed "dirty snowballs". Some comets are only a metre wide. Others are kilometres across. Many comets can be found in distant outer space. This region is called the **Oort Cloud**. It is trillions of kilometres away from the Sun and is cold. This keeps the comets icy. But if a comet comes closer to the Sun, it begins to warm up.

The Oort Cloud is a region that many comets can be found in.

Comet McNaught,
Ashburton, South
Island, New Zealand

When a comet begins to warm up from the Sun, its icy parts turn into gases mixed with dust. These gases reflect the light from the Sun. They form long, bright tails. These tails stretch for millions of kilometres across space. When comets come close enough to Earth, we can see them. They light up the sky.

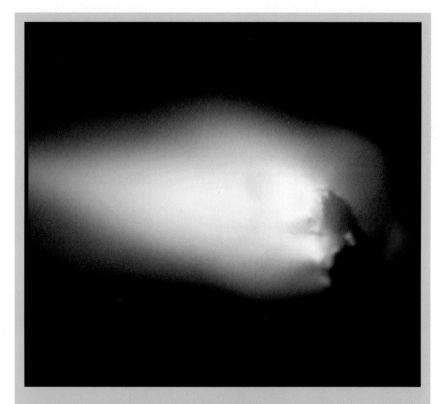

HALLEY'S COMET

Halley's Comet is the world's most famous comet. It is one of the only comets we can see with our naked eyes. Halley's Comet orbits the Sun every 76 years. The next time we will see it is in 2061.

CHAPTER 6

FROM FAR AWAY

In 2017, a mysterious object was discovered floating in space. It was like nothing that had ever been seen in our solar system before. That's because it was actually from another solar system! Scientists named the space object 'Oumuamua. Scientists believe it is mostly made of rock. It had been travelling for millions of years before it reached us. 'Oumuamua was the first object from another solar system to appear in ours. Scientists don't know exactly where it came from. Scientists can learn a lot about other solar systems by studying it.

'Oumuamua was spotted
24 million km (15 million miles)
from Earth.

CHAPTER 7

WHAT IS STILL A MYSTERY?

Scientists are still looking for answers about meteors and meteorites. They believe meteorites could help us understand the beginning of our solar system. Astronomers work every day to learn more about space and all its speeding space rocks. They study fossils of asteroids that landed on Earth a long time ago. These could provide more evidence for the origins of the universe. Studying space objects that landed on Earth can also tell us more about our planet. Scientists have wondered if the water on Earth could have been from an icy comet. But no one knows for sure yet.

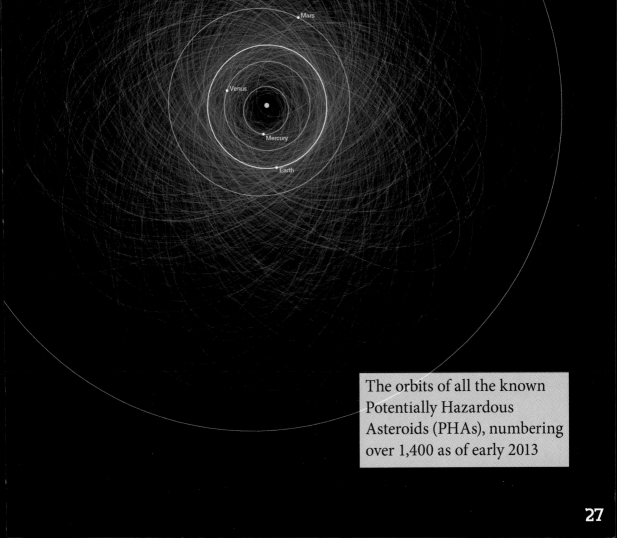

The orbits of all the known
Potentially Hazardous
Asteroids (PHAs), numbering
over 1,400 as of early 2013

Scientists have formed groups to
track asteroids that might hit Earth.

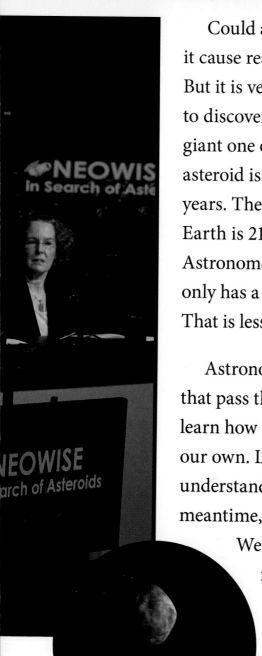

Could an asteroid ever hit Earth again? Could it cause real damage? The short answer is yes. But it is very unlikely. Astronomers are working to discover how to stop an asteroid, especially a giant one on a direct path to Earth. No known asteroid is set to hit our planet in the next 100 years. The next chance for an asteroid to hit Earth is 2185. The asteroid is called Bennu. Astronomers are watching it closely. Still, Bennu only has a one in 2,700 chance of making impact. That is less than a 1 per cent chance! *Phew!*

Astronomers also continue to study the objects that pass through our solar system. We could learn how different other solar systems are from our own. Learning about them could help us understand our solar system better as well. In the meantime, there is one thing we know for sure: We are just beginning to understand the mysteries of space!

Asteroid Bennu

GLOSSARY

asteroid rocky object in space

asteroid belt region of space between Mars and Jupiter where most asteroids are

astronomer someone who studies outer space

atmosphere gases that surround a planet or other objects in space

Big Bang theory that explains how the universe was formed

comet object in space that has dust and gas around it that may form a tail

crater cup-shaped hole in a planet or moon

energy any source of usable power

matter anything that occupies space

meteor meteorid that has entered Earth's atmosphere

meteorite meteoroid that has reached Earth

meteoroid small body of rock travelling through space

Oort Cloud far region in outer space where a lot of comets are

telescope tool people use to look at objects in space

FIND OUT MORE

BOOKS

Meteor: Perspectives on Asteroid Strikes (Disaster Dossiers), Alex Woolf (Raintree, 2015)

The Mysteries of the Universe: Discover the best-kept secrets of space, DK (DK Children, 2020)

Solar System (DKfindout!), Sarah Cruddas (DK Children, 2016)

WEBSITES

www.bbc.co.uk/bitesize/topics/zdrrd2p
Discover more about the solar system.

www.dkfindout.com/uk/space/solar-system/comets
Find out more about comets.

www.esa.int/kids/en/home
Learn more about space from the European Space Agency.

INDEX